THE
SIOUX

Peter Hicks

Thomson Learning • New York

Look into the Past

First published in the
United States in 1994 by
Thomson Learning
115 Fifth Avenue
New York, NY 10003

First published in Great Britain in 1994 by
Wayland (Publishers) Ltd.

Library of Congress Cataloging-in-Publication Data
Hicks, Peter, 1952-
  The Sioux / Peter Hicks.
      p.   cm.—(Look into the past)
  Includes bibliographical references and index.
  ISBN 1-56847-172-6
  1. Dakota Indians—Juvenile literature. [1. Dakota Indians.
2. Indians of North America.]
I. Title. II. Series.
E99.D1H53   1994
978'.004975—dc20   94-1340

Printed Italy

Picture acknowledgments
The publishers wish to thank the following for providing the photographs in this book: Archiv für Kunst und Geschichte, Berlin 23 (bottom); Werner Forman Archive *cover*, 4, 5 (top, Robinson Museum, South Dakota), 6 (Museum für Volkerkunde, Berlin), 7 (all, Plains Indian Museum, Cody, Wyoming), 8 (top, Robinson Museum, bottom Plains Indian Museum), 9 (bottom, Museum of the American Indian, New York), 10, 13 (top, Glenbow Museum, Calgary, Canada), 14 (Plains Indian Museum), 16 (right, Plains Indian Museum), 17 (top, Plains Indian Museum), 20 (both Plains Indian Museum) 22 (left, Museum für Volkerkunde, Berlin), 23 (top, Field Museum of Natural History, Chicago), 24 (British Museum); Peter Newark's Western Americana 5 (bottom), 11 (top), 16 (left), 18, 22 (right), 25 (top), 26; Colin Taylor *cover*, 9 (top), 11 (bottom), 12 (top and bottom/middle), 15 (both), 17 (bottom), 19 (both), 21 (bottom), 27 (both), 28, 29.
Map artwork by Jenny Hughes.

CONTENTS

Words that appear in **bold italic** in the text are explained in the glossary on page 30.

WHO ARE THE SIOUX?

The Sioux, or Dakota Indians to give them their proper name, are a North American Plains nation that descended from the *migrants* who came to the American continent from Asia 30,000 years ago. The name Sioux is actually an insult meaning "little snake," a name given to them by an enemy tribe.

The Sioux first lived just west of the Great ▶ Lakes, but most were pushed west into South Dakota by other tribes. The Eastern, or Santee, Sioux and the Middle, or Nakota, Sioux were hunter-gatherers and farmers. This book concentrates on the Western, or Lakota, Sioux, who were hunter-gatherers and led a *nomadic* life. Many tribes, including the Lakota Sioux, trekked across the plains following the animal they depended upon – the buffalo.

◀ The plains of North America are a huge expanse of grassland that stretches from Texas in the south to Canada in the north and from the Rocky Mountains in the west to about the center of North America to the east. There are some tree-covered hills and mountains and rocky outcrops, but the plains are largely flat.

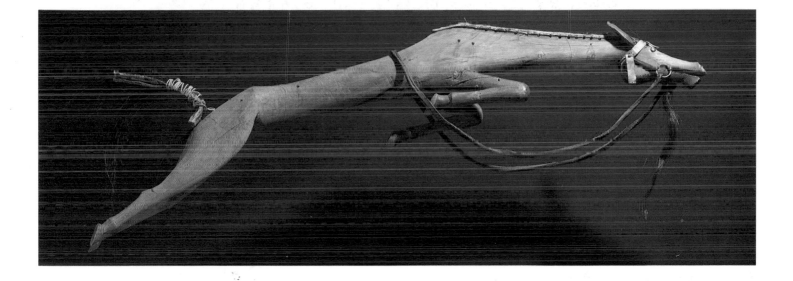

▲ Until the 1600s the Sioux hunted on foot. However, by about 1650 the life of these nomads had changed dramatically. The horse, introduced by the Spanish in South America, reached the Plains tribes. On horseback, the Lakota could hunt buffalo faster and farther afield. This remarkable model shows the power and speed of a war pony. Here was another use of the horse: war parties could swiftly attack neighboring tribes, take them by surprise, and steal their prized possessions – mainly horses.

◀ Because the Lakota were often on the move, they developed a special type of dwelling – the *tepee*. When the tribe broke camp, the tepee, with its soft hide covering stretched over wooden poles, could be taken down very quickly. The poles made up the pony-drawn *travois*, onto which the rolled-up hides and other possessions were fastened. Notice the construction of the tepee: the gap at the top is for venting smoke from the fire.

THE TRIBE AND ITS WAYS

The Lakota Sioux were such a large tribe that they divided up into seven separate bands. The most powerful was the Oglala, which produced such fine and famous warriors as Red Cloud and Crazy Horse. The Lakota's movements depended on the buffalo. In spring and summer many bands joined up to follow the huge grazing herds and kill enough meat for their needs. As well as meat, they ate wild fruits and vegetables, such as cherries, potatoes, onions, and turnips. These were gathered during autumn and stored for the long, harsh winter, which was usually spent camped in sheltered river valleys.

▼ The Lakota's nomadic life made the portable tepee essential. Cooking utensils and containers were also portable. Pottery was useless as it was heavy and likely to break. Most vessels were made of hide, such as the parfleche in this picture. This was a piece of hide that folded like an envelope and was used to carry dried meat and other foods. These highly decorated and prized objects were often presented as gifts. They could be used inside the tepee or as saddlebags.

◄ To the Lakota, marriage and the family were very important. Children were always wanted, particularly males. Because the *death rate* for infants was very high, a newborn baby was always the center of attention. For comfort and ease of movement the infant was wrapped in cotton or moss and securely placed inside a decorated baby carrier. It could easily be strapped to the mother's back, and if the mother was working, the carrier could be hung up to allow the baby to watch her. The designs on the carrier are made by quillwork – the sewing on of beautifully colored porcupine quills. This was considered a great skill.

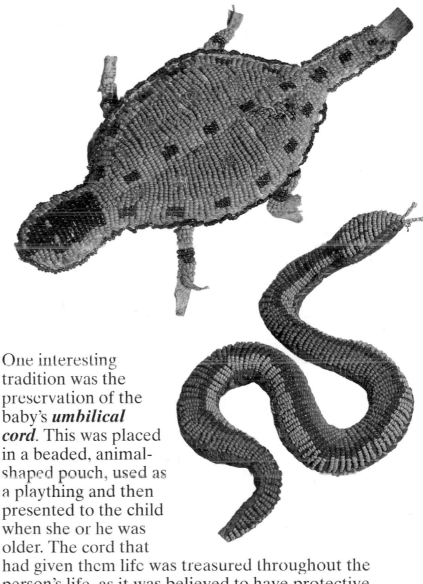

One interesting tradition was the preservation of the baby's *umbilical cord*. This was placed in a beaded, animal-shaped pouch, used as a plaything and then presented to the child when she or he was older. The cord that had given them life was treasured throughout the person's life, as it was believed to have protective powers.

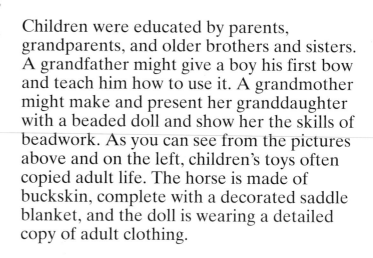

Children were educated by parents, grandparents, and older brothers and sisters. A grandfather might give a boy his first bow and teach him how to use it. A grandmother might make and present her granddaughter with a beaded doll and show her the skills of beadwork. As you can see from the pictures above and on the left, children's toys often copied adult life. The horse is made of buckskin, complete with a decorated saddle blanket, and the doll is wearing a detailed copy of adult clothing.

One *ritual* among Sioux men was the smoking of pipes. This was rarely done only for pleasure, but on occasions of great importance, such as a guest's first visit to the tepee or the final agreement on a friendship or deal. The picture shows a pipe and tobacco bag with quill embroidery and a fringe. ▶

The pipe is very important in the Sioux religion. There are many legends about the most sacred pipe, "the buffalo calf pipe," which is still used for prayer. All pipes have to be blessed, and many people want their pipes blessed by the keeper of the sacred pipe.

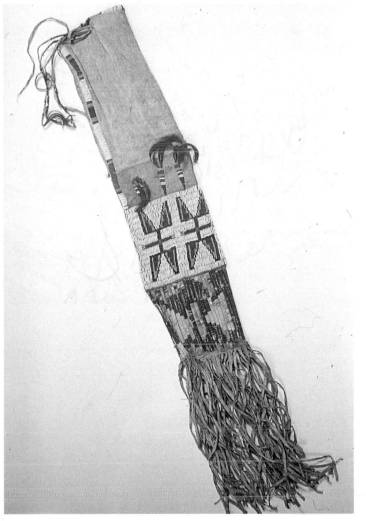

The buffalo calf pipe is said to have been brought by the White Buffalo Woman, a great spirit who was sent by the Buffalo People to stop the warring between the Buffalo and the Sioux, and to ensure that humans would always have food and would increase.

Gifts of pipes or tobacco were highly prized. The wooden pipe stem was often decorated with quills, while the bowl was usually made of a soft stone called pipestone. This special pipe bowl is made of slate. Notice the superbly carved couple and horse's head. ▼

BUFFALO!

Before the introduction of horses to the plains, the Lakota hunted buffalo, or bison, on foot. This was very difficult because of the dangers of large herds running at high speed. Using disguises, such as wolf skins, the hunters had to approach the herd downwind, for buffalo have a very good sense of smell. On these buffalo hunts, the Sioux managed to kill large numbers of animals in ingenious ways.

◄ In winter the hunters drove buffalo into deep snowdrifts and killed them. Also, large numbers were *stampeded* over cliffs like the one in the photograph. In these stampedes, known as the *piskun*, the bison were either killed outright or injured and then picked off at the foot of the cliff. This site has been *excavated* by *archaeologists,* and bison remains and arrowheads dating from A.D. 600 have been found.

▲ Once the horse reached the Americas, the Lakota could kill larger numbers of bison. The mounted hunters charged into the herd, causing a stampede, and were joined by others riding alongside firing arrows and hurling spears. The buffalo hunt, with its noise, dust, and confusion, was still very dangerous. Both horse and rider were in constant danger, for a bull could weigh over 2,000 pounds.

Hunters killed the number of buffalo that ▼ the tribe needed. With specially strengthened bows used only on these hunts, stone- or iron-tipped arrows were fired with great force into the shoulders, necks, and sides of the running bison. The power of these bows was proved by their use long after the introduction of the gun. Their small size – less than one yard long – made them easy to handle, even while riding a pony at full speed.

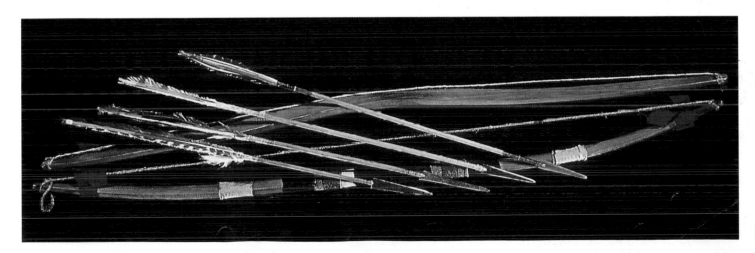

▲ From this scene it is clear that men and women took part in skinning the bison. ***Butchering*** was done with great enthusiasm, for the tribe had secured food for the future. The cut meat would be loaded onto travois and taken to camp. There the best meat might be given to the tribal leaders and other members who helped in the hunt. The rest was either eaten right away or cut into strips, dried, and pounded so it would keep for months. This dried meat was called ***pemmican.***

The woman in the bottom left of this picture is preparing pemmican. Of course, the bison was not used only for food. The hide was very important and had to be specially treated. First the fur and inside fat and tissue had to be scraped off with sharp stones. Then it was stretched and twisted many times before it could be made into items such as tepee covers, belts, shields, ***moccasins***, shirts, and bedcovers. ▶

▲ The rest of the bison *carcass* provided the tribe with many of its raw materials. For example, sinew, the tissue that connects muscle to bone, made bow strings and thread. Horns were shaped into cups and spoons. Bones were used for knives, saddle frames, and shovels (from the shoulder blades). The bison was essential for the Lakota and they honored it constantly. They believed that the buffalo were born from the earth, and that the Great Spirit would always supply them with enough buffalo.

APPEARANCE

Lakota clothing was fairly simple and, with the harsh winters and hot summers of the plains, it varied according to season. In summer, men and women usually wore lighter deer or elk skin and, because of the heat, *tattooing* and personal ornaments replaced a lot of clothing.

◄ Women wore soft skin dresses over knee-length leggings. Look at the dress in the picture. Notice the highly decorated yoke at the top and the fringes on the arms and hem. The yoke was usually made of elks' teeth, shells, and beads.

These women's leggings, with *geometric* quill designs, would have kept the wearer warm in the winter. Men's leggings were ankle-length and loose for comfort on horseback, with a beaded strip up both sides. ▼

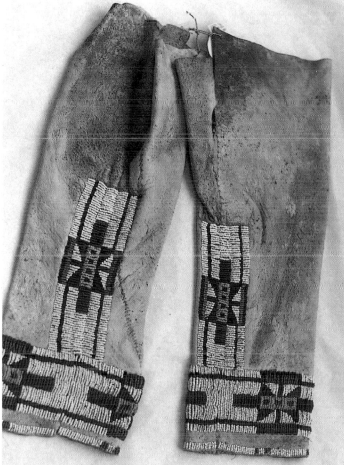

◄ The most important item of clothing was the buffalo robe. Robes made from the hide of young female buffalo were highly prized. For winter wear, the hair was left on, but summer robes were scraped to make them thinner and lighter. Study this robe carefully. Can you find the head and legs of the animal? This robe was worn in winter, with the fur side against the wearer's skin.

Men and women wore their hair in two braids, one on either side of the head. The braids were often decorated with colorful cloth, fur, or beads, which showed the status of the wearer. This is a photograph of Red Shirt, a member of Sitting Bull's Hunkpapa band. Although he is wearing the vest and shirt of the **white man**, notice his long hair and decorations. Around his neck he is wearing the traditional shell choker; he is holding his pipe and tobacco pouch. ▼

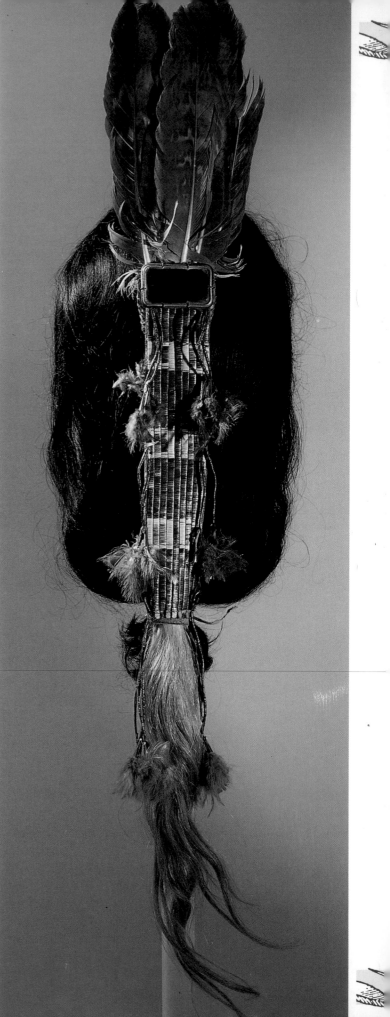

◀ The back of the head was also decorated. This quill and feather hair ornament dates from about 1890. A mirror has been used to keep the feathers in place. Similar mirrors were used to make signals in the wars with the U.S. army. The number of feathers was a mark of the man's war achievements.

The Lakota were ▶ proud of their colorful appearance. These armbands, decorated with quills and feathers, were probably worn during the many ceremonial dances that were held at various times of the year.

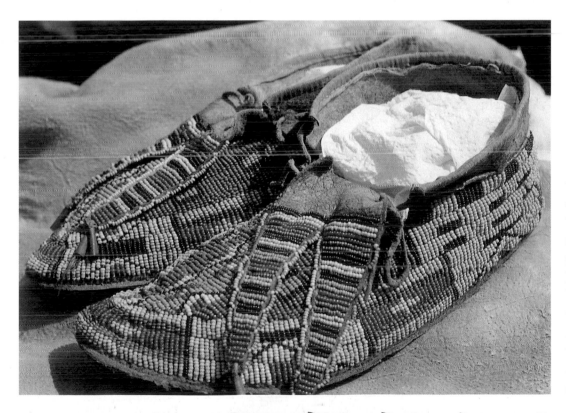

◀ Footwear consisted of moccasins. They were tough and comfortable – the soles were made of hard, untanned buffalo skin, and the uppers from softer, *tanned* hide. They were often lavishly decorated with colorful beads.

WARRIORS

By the nineteenth century the Lakota were a powerful military force. Their warriors on horseback took more land and forced weaker farming tribes to provide them with food. Horse stealing was the main activity between tribes (horses meant wealth), and the Lakota made enemies – particularly the Crow and Pawnee who bordered on their territory. Bows and arrows were important, but other weapons were used in these raids.

One traditional ▶ weapon was the war club. This was a polished, pointed stone head, with a long wooden handle. Buffalo rawhide always shrinks, so this was used to keep the head permanently in place. The long handle would give a mounted warrior a long reach during a fight.

Shields were very ▶ important for many reasons. A well-made, round rawhide shield, perhaps padded with buffalo hair, could stop a swift arrow or an old-fashioned *musket* ball. Shields were decorated with magical paintings showing powerful animals such as eagles or grizzly bears. The power of these animals was thought to pass to the shield's owner. Some warriors were so sure of their powers that they rode into battle with only the shield for cover.

The early guns brought by white traders were not much use to the mounted warriors because they were so difficult to load. However, as guns improved, warriors became interested in owning them. This photograph shows a single-shot Springfield Carbine of 1873 used by the Lakota. With the coming of the repeating rifles, which did not need frequent reloading, the Lakota became even more effective *cavalrymen*. ▶

◄ A brave and skillful warrior was recognized in a number of ways. The eagle-feather war bonnet (above and left) was a sign of a great fighter. The bonnet was made so that when its owner walked, the feathers moved like the eagle in flight – graceful and silent. The size of the bonnet often showed the greatness of a warrior. The feather part of this bonnet is called a trailer, and each eagle feather represents an act of bravery in battle. Clearly, these bonnets were worn by only the most outstanding fighters.

▲ Another sign of a good fighter was the war shirt. Beautifully made in soft deerskin, the wearer would display signs of bravery. The feathers and hair fringes attached to the front and shoulders represented coups (see below), or even the scalps of enemies. Scalping – the removal of the top of an enemy's head and hair – was a sign of total victory. Afterward the scalper "owned" his enemy, because a person's spirit was thought to be in the hair.

◄ An unusual honor in battle was the counting coup. It was considered very brave to ride or run up to an armed enemy and strike him on the head, shoulder, or arm. This would be done with the hand or a special stick. You can see this taking place in the picture. If the blow had been witnessed, the successful warrior would have gained great honor. To have a coup count against you was considered shameful. Look again at the man striking the blow. How can you tell he is a great warrior?

RELIGION AND BELIEFS

Lakota religion was based on all things "wakan," or sacred. Everything in the world came from Wakan Tanka – the Great Spirit, Mystery, or Medicine. After death people would join Wakan Tanka in the afterlife. On Earth he communicated with chosen men, called shaman (which means holy men), who were sometimes called medicine men. They were very important people in the band. Beneath the Great Spirit were four more gods – the Earth, Rock, Sun, and Sky. Beneath these were the lower gods: the Buffalo, Bear, Four Winds, and Whirlwind.

The shaman ▶ was not only the go-between for the band and the Great Spirit, but he also cured illness. He knew herbal remedies for everyday problems like headaches and toothaches. Serious illnesses were more difficult, and he had to receive help from sacred animals like the eagle. This is a shaman's eagle-wing fan, which he used when treating sick people.

▲ The shaman also helped to organize the most important event of the Lakota year – the Sun Dance. Many bands came together, bringing thousands of members for feasting and festivity. The purpose of the dance was to ensure a plentiful supply of buffalo. If it did not take place the herds would disappear and the plants would die. Those chosen for the dance had to offer up pain and suffering, as you can see in the picture. From a central pole came two ropes that were attached to the dancer's chest. The dancer pulled against the ropes until he finally ripped free. The noise from drums and whistles going on for many days made it a dramatic ceremony.

There were many other dances celebrating various events, and these were also opportunities for dressing up. The Night Dance, when partners chose each other, was a great social occasion. The Scalp Dance celebrated victories in battle and the newly won scalps were displayed.

◄ Both the drumming and the singing were central to these ceremonies. Because of their importance, the buffalo and horse figured in many dances. The power of the horse is celebrated on this beautifully painted shirt worn during the "grass in the belt dance," or Grass Dance.

▲ Among the Lakota, death was taken seriously, but was not usually feared by old people. If a child died, relatives would mourn by cutting their flesh and hair and ripping clothing. When a person died the body was usually wrapped with personal objects and placed on a *scaffold* outside the village or in a tree. These burial places were visited and it was known for an older widow to wear the jawbone of her dead husband.

23

WAR AND DEFEAT

During the 1860s the Lakota, led by Red Cloud, went to war with the white man. They hated the roads and forts built on their lands by the U.S. army for the use and protection of gold miners traveling to the Rockies. Red Cloud's war was successful – the government in Washington withdrew the army because of the cost. After the Lakota burned down all the forts a *treaty* was signed. The government agreed to a Great Sioux Reservation – land reserved for the Sioux "as long as the grass shall grow."

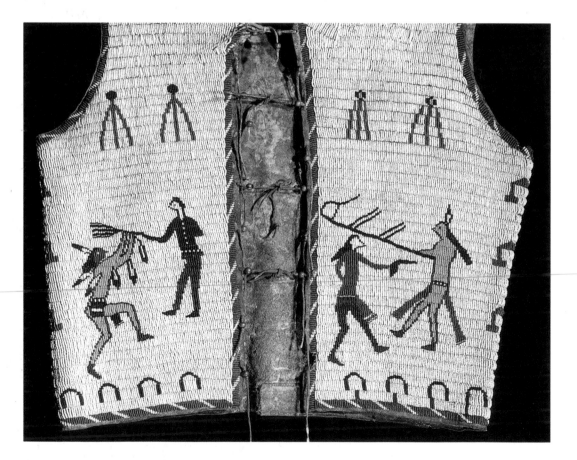

However, by 1874 there were stories that there was gold in the Black Hills – part of the reservation and very sacred to the Lakota. Although whites were not allowed in the Black Hills, a gold rush started and thousands of miners flocked into the area. The Lakota attacked them to defend their homeland. Soon the army was sent in to protect the miners. This beaded jacket shows scenes from the fighting.

The Lakota were ▶ so concerned about this threat that they joined with another tribe, the Cheyenne. The government offered the Lakota $6 million for the Black Hills – far less than the gold alone was worth – but the offer was rejected. War was sure to follow. The head Lakota chief and shaman, Sitting Bull, shown in this picture, had a great vision that many white men would fall into their camp and be killed.

The Lakota and Cheyenne formed a large camp near the Bighorn River in June 1876. The army hoped to encircle this camp and destroy it. General George Armstrong Custer, with more than 600 men, decided to attack without waiting for support. However, Custer and a close group of about 200 soldiers became surrounded by bands of Oglala, Hunkpapa, and Cheyenne. Within one hour Custer and his men were all dead. ▼

Despite this great Sioux victory, the U.S. government was determined to break the power of the Lakota and put them all on reservations. Crazy Horse kept attacking the miners, but when he gave himself up in 1877 he was murdered by the army. The reservations were on the poorest land, yet the whites expected the Sioux to farm. More importantly, the government allowed white hunters to destroy the great buffalo herds. The animal the Sioux most needed for clothing, shelter, and food was disappearing, which made the Lakota dependent on money from the U.S. authorities. ▼

The Lakota hated this life. They were used to a free life, following the buffalo. By 1890 a strange ceremony, called the Ghost Dance (depicted here), swept through the Plains. The dancers clothed themselves in special shirts and robes and entered a *trance*. By dancing, they believed the buffalo would return and the white men leave. The army was called in to stamp out this dance. In one of the skirmishes Sitting Bull was murdered. ▶

Another Lakota chief, Big Foot, wanted by ▶ the army for allowing the Ghost Dance, tried to reach the safety of Red Cloud's reservation. He and more than 300 Lakota were arrested in December 1890 at Wounded Knee. In a scuffle over a gun the army started firing. They killed nearly all the men, women, and children in the band. The bodies of Big Foot and others were left to freeze in the snow. The Lakota never recovered from this *massacre*.

THE SIOUX TODAY

The hundred years since Wounded Knee have been very hard for the Sioux population. They have survived, but at a great cost. For example, early Sioux schools took young children away from their families and tried to make them think and act like whites. They were not allowed to speak their own language or follow the old beliefs. Over the years, Native Americans have become the poorest *ethnic minority* in America. In 1985 there were more than 54,000 Sioux living on reservations in South Dakota alone.

Unfortunately, much reservation housing is poor. Wooden cabins like this one at Standing Rock, North Dakota, rarely have hot and cold running water, electricity, or **sanitation.** Poor housing often leads to poor health, and Native Americans have high rates of diseases such as tuberculosis, diabetes, and dysentery. The infant death rate is high, and Native Americans die much younger than whites. Unemployment is high on the reservations and many Sioux have moved to towns to look for work. Some people feel trapped between the familiar reservation and the unfamiliar towns and cities.

◀ A large number of Sioux make a living from the tourist industry – many people are interested in Native American culture. This display of Sioux clothing is in the Buffalo Bill Historical Center in Wyoming.

Many Sioux feel that things will only get better if education improves. Since 1975 a law has allowed tribes to run their own schools and provide a Sioux *curriculum*. In this way, they can celebrate and protect their history and culture and at the same time come to terms with the modern world. These modern tepees show that Native American traditions have been continued in some areas over the years.

GLOSSARY

Archaeologists   People who study objects and remains from ancient times.

Butchering   Cutting up a dead animal into pieces that can be used as meat.

Carcass   The dead body of an animal.

Cavalrymen   Soldiers who fight on horseback.

Curriculum   A course of study at school.

Death rate   The number of deaths out of a certain group in a particular area or age range.

Ethnic minority   A group of people of one race or nationality who share a culture, but live in a country where most of the other people share a different culture.

Excavate   To dig up buried remains.

Geometric   A pattern made up of regular shapes.

Massacre   The fierce killing of large numbers of people.

Migrants   People who move from one country or part of the world to another.

Moccasins   Shoes made from soft leather.

Musket   A long-barreled gun that fired single lead balls.

Nomadic   Describing nomads, people who do not have particular homes, but move from place to place.

Pemmican   A small pressed cake of shredded, dried meat, pounded into paste with fat and berries.

Ritual   A set way of performing a ceremony.

Sanitation   The use of proper cleaning arrangements to protect health.

Scaffold   A raised wooden platform.

Stampeded   Scared a herd of animals into running in one direction.

Tanned   The way animal hide is treated to turn it into leather.

Tattooing   Making designs or pictures on the skin by pricking it and staining it with color.

Tepee   A conical tent usually made from animal skins. In the Dakota language, *ti* means "to dwell" and *pi* means "used for."

Trance   A sleeplike state.

Travois   A type of sled made with two poles in a frame that was pulled by an animal.

Treaty   A formal agreement between two or more states or countries.

Umbilical cord   The long cord that connects a baby to its mother before it is born.

White man   White settlers who ruled the U.S.

IMPORTANT DATES

around 30,000 B.C. First migrants reach North America from Asia

up to A.D. 1400s Sioux settle in the headwaters of the Mississippi

A.D. 1500s Sioux migrate to plains after war with the Cree

1519 The Spanish, led by Cortés, introduce the horse to America

1600s The horse reaches the plains

1841 First wagon trains trek across the plains

1866 Red Cloud's war against the U.S. army begins

1868 Red Cloud signs Laramie Treaty; Huge Lakota reservation set up

1874 Gold rush to the Black Hills on the Lakota reservation, bringing in thousands of white miners

1875 Lakota and Cheyenne join forces for Summer Sun Dance

1876 U.S. army campaign against Lakota and Cheyenne begins
Lakota and Cheyenne victory at the Battle of Little Bighorn
General Custer killed, June 25

1877 Lakota surrender to U.S. army. They lose Powder River County and the Black Hills
September: Crazy Horse murdered

1889 Break up of the Great Lakota reservation

1890 October-November: Ghost Dance sweeps the plains
December: Sitting Bull murdered, Massacre at Wounded Knee

BOOKS TO READ

Flint, David. *The Prairies and Their People*. People and Places. New York: Thomson Learning, 1994.

Hoover, Herbert T. *Yankton Sioux*. New York: Chelsea House, 1988.

Landau, Elaine. *The Sioux*. First Books. New York: Franklin Watts, 1989.

Liptak, Karen. *North American Indian Ceremonies*. First Books. New York: Franklin Watts, 1992.

May, Robin. *Plains Indians of North America*. Vero Beach, FL: Rourke Corp., 1987.

Nicholson, Robert. *The Sioux*. New York: Chelsea House, 1994.

Smithsonian Institution Press. *Handbook of the North American Indian*. An ongoing series divided geographically.

Wilson, James. *Native Americans*. Threatened Cultures. New York: Thomson Learning, 1994.

INDEX

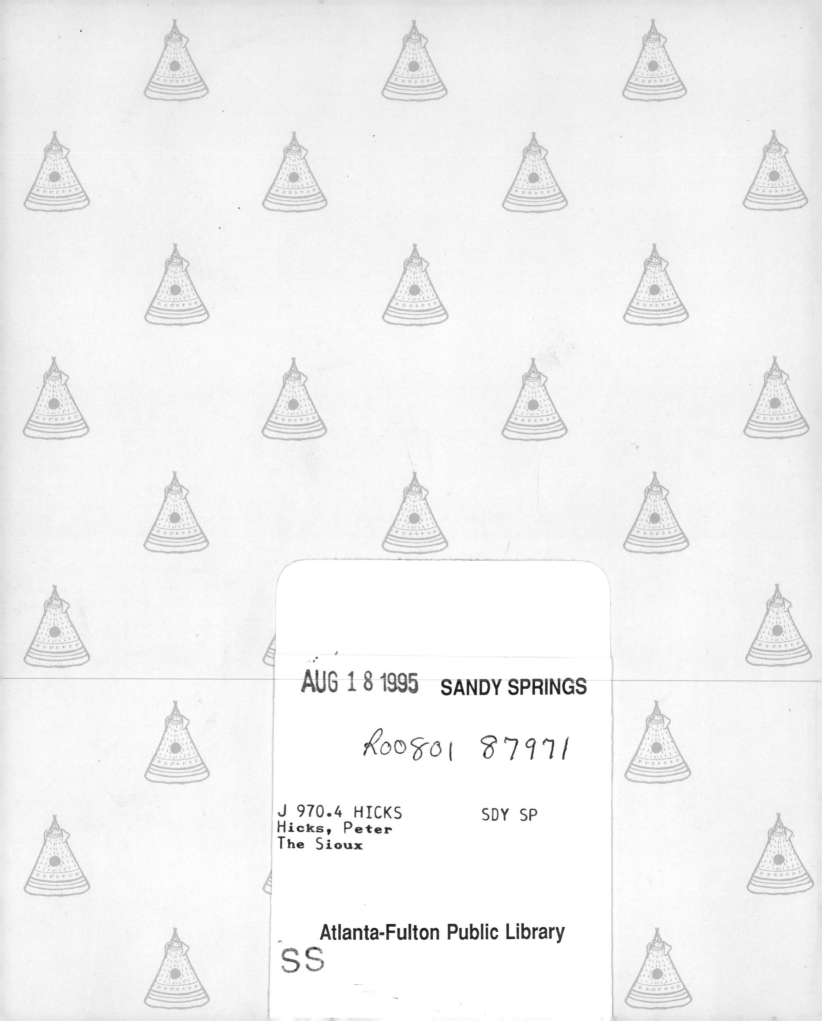